About This Book

Title: *Crabs*

Step: 2

Word Count: 111

Skills in Focus: R-blends

Tricky Words: live, far, sea, claws, fresh, food, cook, shell, eat, prey

Ideas For Using This Book

Before Reading:

- **Comprehension:** Look at the title and cover image together. Walk through the pictures in the book with readers and have them make predictions about what they might learn in the book. Help them make connections by asking what they already know about crabs.
- **Accuracy:** Practice saying the tricky words listed on page 1.
- **Phonemic Awareness:** Explain to readers that a blend is two consonants together that each make a sound. Discuss that some blends include the letter *r*. Read aloud story words containing r-blends, beginning with *crab*. Segment the sounds in the word slowly and have the students call out the word. Call attention to each blend and where it is found within the word.

During Reading:

- Have readers point under each word as they read it.
- **Decoding:** If readers are stuck on a word, help them say each sound and blend the sounds together smoothly. Be sure to point out r-blends as they appear.
- **Comprehension:** Invite students to talk about what new things they are learning about crabs while reading. What are they learning that they didn't know before?

After Reading:

Discuss the book. Some ideas for questions:

- What did you learn about where crabs live and what they look like?
- Have you ever eaten crab? Would you like to try it?
- What do you still wonder about crabs?

Crabs

Text by Marley Richmond

Reading Consultant
Deborah MacPhee, PhD
Professor, School of Teaching and Learning
Illinois State University

PICTURE WINDOW BOOKS
a capstone imprint

Crabs can live in the sea.

Crabs can live on sand.

Crabs can be in grass.

Crabs in grass are not far from the sea.

Crabs can be brick red.

Crabs can be black.
They can have spots.

A crab can grab and grip with its claws.

A crab can clap its claws.

A crab grabs food with its claws.

A crab can grasp prey.
It can drag the prey.

Crabs can be food
when they are fresh.

Crabs swim to traps.

A crew picks up the traps.
The traps are full of crabs.
You can cook crabs.

Press on cooked crabs
to crack the shell.
You can eat the crab.

More Ideas:

Phonics and Phonemic Awareness Activity

Practicing R-Blends:

Play I Spy! Prepare word cards with consonant blend story words. Place each card face up on a surface. Choose a word to start the game. Say "I spy" and then segment the sounds in the word. For example, "I spy /c/, /r/, /a/, /b/." The readers will call out the word and then look for the corresponding card. Continue until all cards have been collected.

Suggested words:

- crab
- grab
- grip
- grass
- crack
- press

Extended Learning Activity

Let's Draw!

Show readers pictures of crabs. Ask them to count how many legs the crabs have. Then ask readers to draw a picture of a crab. Have them draw the crab's legs. Ask readers to write down a word or phrase to describe the crab along each leg. Challenge readers to use words with r-blends.

Published by Picture Window Books, an imprint of Capstone
1710 Roe Crest Drive, North Mankato, Minnesota 56003
capstonepub.com

Library of Congress Cataloging-in-Publication Data is available on the Library of Congress website.

ISBN: 9798875227035 (hardback)
ISBN: 9798875229596 (paperback)
ISBN: 9798875229572 (eBook PDF)

Photo Credits: iStock: ChristiLaLiberte, 20–21, lengel76, 1, 13, Martin Leber, 16–17, Mlenny, 10, preuk13, 22–23, RainervonBrandis, 12, 24, stu99, 19, Wirestock, 4; Shutterstock: AlexMattison, 11, Art Sublimina Photography, 8–9, Gidon Pico, 6–7, Jan Jenka, 2–3, Maya Rubinstein, cover, MoritzAfrica, 5, Olga Popova, 18, valda butterworth, 14–15

Printed and bound in China. 6274